Contents

Introduction 4

How do we know? 6

Blitzkrieg! 8

The Battle of Britain 10

The Blitz 12

Pearl Harbor 14

Fighting in Africa 16

The fall of Singapore 18

The Soviet defence 20

Fighting in the Philippines 22

The enemy below 24

Women at war 26

War in the Pacific 28

Defending Australia 30

Advancing through Italy 32

D-Day 34

Air raids on Germany 36

The Battle of the Bulge 38

The Holocaust 40

Through Burma 42

Yalta 44

V-E Day 46

The atomic bomb 48

What have we learnt from World War II? 50

Timeline 52

Find out more 53

List of primary sources 53

Glossary 54

Index 56

Introduction

World War II was the most destructive war in human history. It cost millions of lives, made millions more homeless and left many countries crushed by its economic cost. It was also the first 'modern' war – armed forces today still use many of the type of weapons that first saw action during World War II. In addition, the sights and sounds of the fighting were brought to people's homes thanks to radio, telephone and modern newspaper communications.

How it happened

During the 1930s the **Nazi** Party in Germany (led by Adolf Hitler), Benito Mussolini's Italian **fascists** and the military leaders of Japan (led by General Hideki Tojo and swearing loyalty to Emperor Hirohito) believed that their countries deserved to have more land and power. Germany wanted to regain its national pride after the disastrous effects of its defeat in World War I. Japan needed access to more natural resources to become a major economic power. Treaties signed between these countries in 1936–37 brought into being the Rome–Berlin–Tokyo **Axis**. From that point on, they were referred to as the Axis powers.

Although the aggressive aims of the Axis powers seemed to point towards another war, few countries welcomed another major conflict like World War I. Many people in Great Britain, for example, wanted a policy of **appeasement** towards Hitler. Also, many Americans wanted no part of another 'European dispute'; this **isolationism** would continue even after World War II was under way.

The war itself began in September 1939 when Germany invaded Poland. Great Britain and France, the first countries to be known as the **Allied** powers, immediately declared war on Germany. The well-prepared Germans soon defeated Poland. Some observers believed that Germany's advance would stop there, especially during the quiet months that followed. The British press described this period as the 'Phoney War', but it ended abruptly when German forces swept westward across northern Europe the following spring. France itself was defeated in 1940, and by then most of western Europe was controlled by the Axis powers (see map on page 8).

Witness to History

World War II

Sean Connolly

www.heinemann.co.uk/library
Visit our website to find out more information about **Heinemann Library** books.

To order:
 Phone 44 (0) 1865 888066
Send a fax to 44 (0) 1865 314091
Visit the Heinemann Bookshop at www.heinemann.co.uk/library to browse our catalogue and order online.

First published in Great Britain by Heinemann Library,
Halley Court, Jordan Hill, Oxford
OX2 8EJ, part of Harcourt Education.
Heinemann is a registered trademark of Harcourt
Education Ltd.

© Harcourt Education Ltd 2003
First published in paperback in 2004
The moral right of the proprietor has been asserted.

Editorial: Sarah Eason and Kathy Peltan
Design: Ron Kamen and Celia Floyd
Illustrations: Stefan Chabluk
Picture Research: Maria Joannou
Production: Viv Hichens.

Originated by Ambassador Litho Ltd
Printed and bound in Hong Kong, China by
South China Printing

ISBN 0 431 17033 9 (hardback)
07 06 05 04
10 9 8 7 6 5 4 3 2

ISBN 0 431 17039 8 (paperback)
08 07 06 05 04
10 9 8 7 6 5 4 3 2 1

British Library Cataloguing in Publication Data
Connolly, Sean, 1956–
  World War II. – (Witness to History)
  1. World War, 1939–1945 – Juvenile literature
  I. Title
  940.5

A full catalogue record for this book is available from the
British Library.

Acknowledgements
The publishers would like to thank the following for
permission to reproduce photographs:
AKG Photos p.**7**; Colin Perry p.**13**; Collections/Michael
Diggin p.**25**; Hulton Archive pp.**12**, **23**, **26**, **35**, **41**, **47**;
Illustrated London News p.**44**; Imperial War
Museum/Camera Press p.**32**; Patrick Connolly pp.**29**, **39**;
Popperfoto p.**48**; Topham p.**11**; Topham Picturepoint pp.**10**,
18, **22**, **31**, **38**, **43**, **46**, **51**; Topham Picturepoint/Associated
Press pp.**5**, **15**, **21**; pp. **9**, **17**, **20**, **24**, **28**, **36** unknown.

Cover photograph of the aftermath of a bombing raid in
Germany, April 1945. Reproduced with permission of
Hulton Archive.

The publishers would like to thank Bob Rees, historian and
Assistant Head Teacher, for his assistance in the
preparation of this book.

Words appearing in bold, **like this,** are explained in the Glossary.

In 1941 Germany invaded the Soviet Union. Later that year Japan attacked much of British-controlled Asia as well as the US Pacific **fleet** in Hawaii (see pages 14–15). The United States then entered the war as one of the Allies, fighting the Japanese in the Pacific and sending troops to fight in Europe. By early 1942, however, the Axis powers had made great gains.

After two years of fierce fighting, the Allies turned the tide of the war. Soviet troops drove the Germans out of their country and the Japanese were losing their Pacific conquests, island by island. In June 1944 the Allies launched the D-Day attack on German-controlled France (see pages 34–35). They then pushed east towards Germany and north from Italy – Italy had surrendered in 1943. Germany and Japan came under constant attack. Allied troops declared victory in Europe on 8 May 1945 (see pages 46–47). The Japanese held out for another three months until they too surrendered in August 1945 (see pages 48–49).

Bombing raids on the German city of Dresden by American and British forces killed more than 30,000 people and destroyed around 75,000 homes.

How do we know?

By studying history, we can learn about the events of the past. If we need to find out about, for example, the fall of the Roman Empire or the Norman invasion of England, we can find many books and articles about these subjects. They can tell us when and how these events took place, as well as who were the leading characters. They often explain why things have happened, by giving the background to the events, and also describe how the events themselves changed the course of history.

Although these works are informative, they are often written many years – sometimes many centuries – after the events occurred. Like any story that is told, some changes can creep in. Perhaps the historian did not like French people, or Romans, or military leaders generally. That attitude of mind can affect how the story gets told, because the historian wants to present the facts as he or she wanted them to occur. Perhaps the historian might leave out some of the facts that do not fit into this view. Such a personal opinion is called **bias**, and it makes some historical accounts unreliable.

Of course, a historian might have no personal opinion on the matter, but still may use other accounts that were written long after the events. Such accounts are called **secondary sources**, because the historian arrives at them second-hand. Again we must take care in deciding on the truth. The second historian, using earlier retellings, might be repeating the bias or even mistakes of the previous accounts. Each retelling increases the risk of bias and inaccuracy.

Getting to the source

This book aims to use **primary sources** to tell the story of World War II. These are the first-hand accounts of events. Historians dealing with events of long ago must rely on written primary sources: codes of law, parish registers, letters and sometimes journals or diaries. World War II is much more recent and there are many people alive today who lived through the period. So historians can use a much wider range of primary sources to get at the truth of this story. Tape recordings, on-line interviews and film footage of events add to the wealth of written material about this terrible war.

When the Nazis occupied the Netherlands they persecuted the Jews. In 1942, Anne Frank, a Jewish girl, went into hiding along with her family for two years until they were captured. The diary she kept while in hiding gives us a vivid account of her experiences. Anne died in a **Nazi concentration camp** in 1945.

Making our minds up

Of course, not every primary source is without bias and that is true of some of the sources you will find in this book. Personal diaries and accounts tell the truth, but only so far as the writer can know it. The diary accounts of the **Blitz** (see pages 12–13) or the fall of Singapore (see pages 18–19) were written by ordinary people who had no part to play in the planning. Other accounts, although written by eyewitnesses, were meant to urge their countryfolk to victory. General Rommel's description of the fall of France (see pages 8–9) or the *Daily Telegraph* report of a British advance in North Africa (see pages 16–17) are examples of such **propaganda**. By recognizing the shortcomings of such primary sources we can judge them and use them wisely to piece together the complicated jigsaw puzzle that is World War II.

Blitzkrieg!

Hitler's invasion of Poland triggered the start of World War II in September 1939. After the 'Phoney War' – a quiet period that lasted through the following winter – Germany was once more on the attack. The German strategy of *blitzkrieg* ('lightning war'), using air power and speed, allowed Hitler's forces to sweep across northern Europe. Belgium and the Netherlands fell quickly in spring 1940, but the main German target was France. The French were relying on a series of forts and gun emplacements along their border with Germany, known as the Maginot Line, to fight off any German attack.

But the Maginot Line had been built with World War I fighting in mind – the French had expected thousands of German foot soldiers to attack. In the face of air strikes and fast-moving Panzer tanks, it proved to be almost worthless. France fell to the Germans in June 1940. Great Britain was now the only threat to Hitler's advance, and Germany began to concentrate its forces along France's western shores.

Axis nations

Nations and areas controlled by Axis powers

Allied nations occupied by Axis powers

Nations and areas controlled by Soviet Union

Allied nations occupied by Soviet Union

Allied nations and nations and areas under Allied control

Neutral nations

Vichy France and nations under Vichy control

By 1940 Germany had overrun much of Western Europe and created a separate territoty in southern France. This was under the control of the Vichy government loyal to the Axis powers. Later, in 1941, Hitler invaded Greece and Yugoslavia. The Germans then advanced into the Soviet Union.

General Rommel's journal

General Erwin Rommel led Germany's 7th Panzer Division as it crashed through the Belgian defences into France, after German forces had broken through the Maginot Line further south. Here, in an excerpt from his journal, he describes the action on 16 May 1940.

The tanks now rolled in a long column through the line of fortifications and on towards the first houses, which had been set alight by our fire. Occasionally an enemy machine-gun or anti-tank gun fired, but none of their shots came anywhere near us. Our artillery was dropping heavy harassing fire on villages and the road far ahead of the regiment. Gradually the speed increased. Before long we were into the fortified zone. Engines roared, tank tracks clanked and clattered. Whether or not the enemy was firing was impossible to tell in the ear-splitting noise. We crossed the railway line a mile or so south-west of Solre le Chateau, and then swung north to the main road which was soon reached. Then off along the road and past the first houses.

Panzer tank units smashed through defences and moved quickly, destroying enemy villages and supplies. They played a vital part in German *blitzkrieg* tactics.

The people in the houses were rudely awoken by the din of our tanks, the clatter and roar of tracks and engines. Troops lay **bivouacked** beside the road, military vehicles stood parked in farmyards and in some places on the road itself. Civilians and French troops, their faces distorted with terror, lay huddled in the ditches, alongside hedges and in every hollow beside the road.

The Battle of Britain

By June 1940, with most of Europe now defeated, Germany turned its attention to its one remaining enemy – Great Britain. Invasion was the best way to crush Britain, but first Germany had to destroy the Royal Air Force (RAF). In August 1940 the Germans launched a series of daylight air raids. They hoped to draw out RAF fighters and destroy them. British fighters did take on the Germans and, thanks to the new invention of **radar**, they gained an edge in tracking down enemy aircraft. The RAF gradually gained control of the skies.

Most of this **aerial** combat took place over south-east England, closest to Germany's air bases on the continent. British civilians watched this 'Battle of Britain' unfold from the ground, cheering as each German plane was shot down. The RAF crews were recognized as heroes. By September 1940 Hitler decided that the battle to defeat Britain's air force was lost.

Spitfires patrolling the skies over south-east England tried to chase off or shoot down enemy planes.

Hubert Banner's account

Hubert S. Banner describes how he and his wife, living in Kent during the Battle of Britain, saw their first German airman.

'**Never in the field of human conflict was so much owed by so many to so few.**'
(British Prime Minister, Winston Churchill, speaking in Parliament as the Battle of Britain peaked on 20 August 1940.)

A German Messerschmitt chases a Spitfire. Fighter planes would weave and dive through the clouds, often cheered on by crowds watching below.

I saw my first Nazi at close quarters during those memorable days. My wife and I had just finished lunch when we were startled by a 'zoom' that ended in a loud crash. Rushing to the window, we saw a column of black smoke rising above the treetops, and a few moments later began a crackling **fusillade** that reminded one of the Fifth of November. We jumped into the car and drove towards the smoke and noise, and soon we were overtaking a throng of cyclists and pedestrians heading in the same direction.

The scene of the crash was on a golf course, and a good-sized crowd had arrived there before us. The German fighter-bomber had hit the tree tops on its descent, and there it lay, sprawling broken-backed on the greensward. It was consuming rapidly in its own flames, and the empty cartridge cases leapt out of the **pyre** in all directions. The police had formed a **cordon**.

Beneath the trees lay the Nazi airman. A first-aid party was in attendance. Tender hands were bandaging his forehead and broken leg. He was silent now, but I learned afterwards that when first dragged from his burning plane he had made noise enough until one of them said to him, 'Be a man and shut up, can't you? You asked for it, and now you've got it.' Not another squeak had come from him after that...

11

The Blitz

On 7 September 1940, the German bombers launched their first large-scale attack on a British city – London. From then on they launched devastating attacks on Britain's cities, night after night, 'area bombing' the cities and their people.

The period from September 1940 to May 1941 is known as the **Blitz**, from the German word *blitzkrieg* – lightning war. What made the Blitz (and the British bombings of German cities which followed) so shocking was that it was **civilians**, not factories or military buildings, that were the targets. The Luftwaffe (German Air Force) bombed busy ports and industrial cities, like London, Hull and Liverpool. The most destructive raid was on the city of Coventry on the night of 14–15 November 1940. Among the buildings destroyed or severely damaged were more than three-quarters of the city's factories and Coventry Cathedral.

The Blitz was intended to **demoralize** the British people, to make them less able to resist invasion. It did have a huge impact on people's lives. Many Londoners took to sheltering in Underground stations; some of them spent almost all their time there.

About 43,000 civilians were killed by German bombing of Britain's cities. Many more were made homeless. Although the people of Britain suffered, more than 750,000 German civilians were killed during the war.

Colin Perry's diary

Colin Perry, aged 18, lived in Wandsworth, London during the Blitz. He kept his diary from March to November 1940. It tells us about the suffering caused to ordinary people. It also shows the determination people had to withstand the Blitz. This entry is dated 25 September 1940.

Colin Perry with Prime Minister Churchill on 10 September 1940. Churchill was surveying the devastation caused by the Blitz in central London.

The alarm was given early, and until 10.30 we had a great deal of gunfire and bombs, in which period some fell exceedingly close. After 10.30 we had a comparative quiet period and Dad and I retired to bed. I was awakened by Dad calling at me to go in the hall at a quarter-to-one this morning. Above, an enormous number of enemy planes were roaring; our guns spoke I don't know how many times to the second. Great powerful guns just near us.

Suddenly there came a whistle, shrill, followed by another nearer, yet a third, this time seemingly on top of us. Bombs! As they thudded down whistling, and then sudden silence, another **salvo** descended, and the fourth fell the other side of our flat, so did a fifth and sixth. In other words a stick of bombs had straddled our building. Well, we got back into bed, and without exaggeration it was undoubtedly our busiest night. I was awakened almost hourly, and lay listening to the roar of jockeying planes, the scream of bombs, and the terrific noise of our guns which vibrated in my ears. I looked out – fires, searchlights, shells – a **pandemonium**.

Pearl Harbor

The United States had remained outside of the war for more than two years because of a widespread feeling of **isolationism**. Even so, it supported Great Britain in many ways. It offered the British loans to help in their war effort, and even sent warships and ammunition. Meanwhile, the world felt that it was only a matter of time before the Americans would actually join the fighting on the side of the **Allies**.

Japan knew that the massive US Pacific fleet would be a major threat once America did enter the war, so it decided to strike a blow to destroy American naval power. The Japanese believed that they themselves would be too powerful to defeat by the time the US fleet was rebuilt. On the morning of 7 December 1941, Japanese submarines and carrier-based planes attacked the US Pacific fleet at Pearl Harbor, Hawaii. Eighteen American warships (including eight battleships) were sunk or badly damaged, about 200 American aircraft were destroyed, and 3000 sailors and soldiers were killed or wounded. On 8 December President Franklin Roosevelt described the attack as 'a day that will live in **infamy**' and announced that the United States had declared war against Japan. On 11 December Germany declared war on the US.

The Japanese planned to control all the Pacific islands after bombing US battleships in Pearl Harbor.

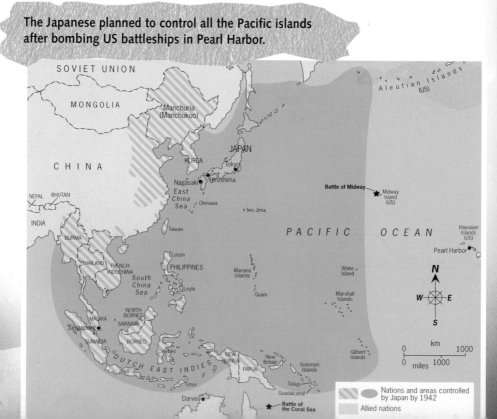

George Phraner's experience
George Phraner was a sailor on board the USS *Arizona*, one of
the battleships destroyed on 7 December 1941. Here he
describes the first terrifying moments of the attack, which
began just after he had finished breakfast.

At first, we didn't realize it was a bombing. It didn't mean anything to us until a large group of planes came near the ship and we could see for the first time the rising sun emblem on the plane wings. The bombing was becoming heavier all around us and we knew this was REALLY IT! At first there was a rush of fear, the blood started to flow real fast. There we were, the Japanese dropping bombs over us and we had no ammo. Somehow the gun captain pointed at me and said, 'you go **aft** and start bringing up the ammunition out of the **magazines**'. The aft magazines were five decks below. A few moments later I found myself deep below the water line in a part of the ship I normally would never be in... I had begun lifting shells into the hoist when a deafening roar filled the room and the entire ship shuddered. It was the forward magazine. One and a half million pounds of gunpowder exploding in a massive fireball disintegrating the whole forward part of the ship. Only moments before I stood with my gun crew just a few feet from the center of the explosion. Admiral Kidd, Captain Van Velkenburg, my whole gun crew was killed.
Everyone on top.

Japanese torpedoes and bombs attack the USS *Arizona*. More than 1000 crewmen were trapped and died inside the ship.

Fighting in Africa

North Africa was the scene of fierce fighting during World War II. British-controlled Egypt had the vital Suez Canal linking Europe with Asia. Much-needed oil from the Middle East could be shipped through the Canal. Italian and German forces, based in the Italian colony of Libya, attacked the British in Egypt and won some important battles in June and July 1942. The British Eighth Army was driven back to El Alamein in Egypt. The Germans were led by General Erwin Rommel, who had swept through France two years before (see pages 8–9). Rommel's successes in North Africa earned him the nickname 'The Desert Fox'.

In October 1942 General Montgomery began to mount a British **counter-attack**. On 23 October British guns at El Alamein began blasting **Axis** positions to prepare for the actual attack. Within two weeks the British had broken through the German and Italian lines, forcing them back into Libya. The battle ended a string of North African victories for Hitler and became a turning point in the war.

Victory at El Alamein allowed Montgomery's Eighth Army to pursue Rommel's troops across Northern Libya, securing the entire coast for the **Allies**.

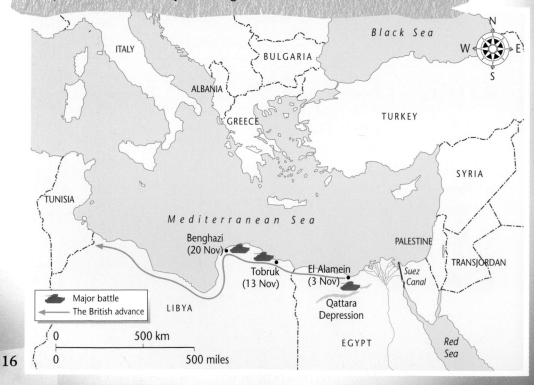

A war correspondent's report

This report from a *Daily Telegraph* war **correspondent** (dated 26 October 1942) describes the devastating first phase of the Battle for El Alamein.

From Christopher Buckley
With the Eighth Army, Sunday

All who witnessed agree that the **artillery** barrage which preceded Gen. Montgomery's opening attack was comparable in intensity with those terrible hurricanes of shell fire which lashed the trenches of the Western Front in the last war. It was precisely 9.40 on Friday night that, with a crash and flash all round the horizon, the British burst into life. It was an awe inspiring experience.

RAF pilots say that the whole front was ablaze with bursting shells, **tracers** and burning vehicles for 30 miles from the sea to Qattara. The Allied air forces are keeping up the terrific blasting of the enemies' positions which has been a feature of the past fortnight.

General Montgomery led the British forces in North Africa from August 1942. Although the British government wanted him to rush into an attack, he made sure his troops were fully prepared before going into battle.

In a Special Order of the Day to the Eighth Army Gen. Montgomery called on his men to 'destroy Rommel and his Army'. With large numbers of well-trained reinforcements from home, he declared 'victory should swing our way'.

Tonight British tanks and infantry are battling furiously within the Axis lines at several points between El Alamein and the Qattara Depression. A number of prisoners have been taken.

Although the Eighth Army's big attack, launched under the full moon at 10 p.m. on Friday, has been held up at some places, a number of definite gaps have been forced in the enemy's closely packed minefields. At one point our tanks broke through in some strength.

The fall of Singapore

At the start of World War II much of Asia (including what are now India, Pakistan, Sri Lanka, Bangladesh, Malaysia, Hong Kong and Singapore) formed part of the British Empire. Great Britain knew it could use this territory as a defence against Japanese attack. The Asian parts of the empire were also important sources of rubber and oil, both vital for Britain's war effort.

The island of Singapore, situated at the base of the Malay peninsula in south-east Asia, had to be well defended. If Singapore was overrun it would make the rest of Asia easier to attack. A **causeway** linked it to the mainland, but the British believed that the danger came from the seas to the south and east. Massive guns pointed out to sea, threatening any possible invader who chose to attack.

The Japanese made a surprise attack by land. They made their way south through the dense jungle of the Malay peninsula, storming Singapore and capturing this island-city on 15 February 1942. It was, said British Prime Minister Winston Churchill, the worst defeat suffered by Britain's army.

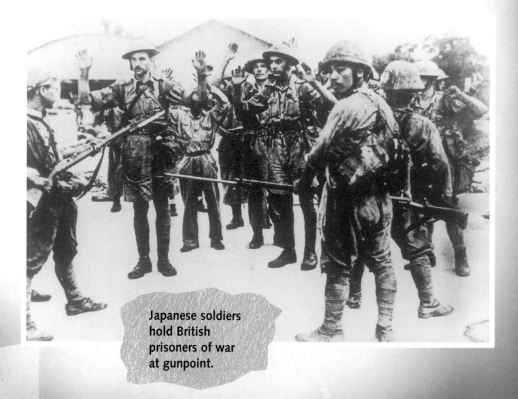

Japanese soldiers hold British prisoners of war at gunpoint.

Victor Bruce's diary

Victor Neville Bruce was an Australian sailor on the HMAS *Bendigo*, which was docked in Singapore Harbour at the time of the Japanese invasion. His diary entries tell of the violence and confusion of that period.

31-1-42	Usual formation of 27 planes bomb aerodrome. The **siege** of Singapore Island starts tonight. The causeway was blown up today.
1-2-42	Anchored in Keppel Harbour. Average of 8 or 9 raids a day.
2-2-42	Closest shave of the war, 18 Jap bombers straddle us with bombs [2 on port side 2 starboard and a couple astern] and hide the ship in spray, shrapnel flew everywhere and pierced Captain's Lobby [steel] door and dented ship's side in several places.
3-2-42	Another severe **blitz** on the docks, dead piled into lorries and carted away. Docks heavily bombed and the raid lasted for two hours. Smell from the wharves is terrible owing to decomposition of bodies under debris.
4-2-42	Usual 27 bombers drop eggs [slang for bombs] among crowded merchant shipping holing several and severely wounding four of the crew of a Naval Auxiliary vessel. Shrapnel fell on X deck. Near the two pounder [gun]. Docks smell like a **charnel house** as many bodies are still under debris, and decomposition sets in quickly in this climate. The Japs have a clear field now, as our Air Force is nil, but five or six Tomahawks arrived from Batavia [Jakarta, Indonesia], with American pilots.
5-2-42	Usual 27 overhead and bombed the docks, and we watched dive bombers at work for some time until a message came through to weigh anchor immediately and proceed to a stricken troop ship.

The Soviet defence

The Soviet Union opposed nearly everything about Nazi Germany in the 1930s, but it did not feel strong enough to defend itself. In order to 'buy time' to build up its military forces, it signed a Non-Aggression agreement with Germany in August 1939. In 1941, however, the Soviet Union was plunged into the war and into alliance with the Allied powers when Germany broke the terms of the agreement and invaded. The Germans got to within 28 km (17 miles) of the capital, Moscow. They virtually surrounded the country's second-largest city, Leningrad, in September 1941 and began a **siege**. More than a million people in the city died over the next 900 days, as supplies of food and fuel dwindled to next to nothing. A lucky few succeeded in making a daring escape across the frozen surface of Lake Ladoga.

Some of the worst fighting of the war took place in the Soviet Union. Many experts say that the turning point in the war came in February 1943, when Soviet forces defeated the Germans at the Battle of Stalingrad. That victory gave the Soviet people – and all of the **Allies** – hope. Slowly the Soviet forces began pushing the Germans westward from their country, but all this came with a huge price. Historians now believe that over 20 million Soviet people died during the war.

Soviet troops were well prepared for the harsh Soviet winter. The Germans lacked warm clothing and many suffered from frostbite.

Lyudmila Anopova's description
Lyudmila Anopova was eight years old when the Siege of Leningrad began. Recollecting the siege in 1944, she describes how small things can sometimes worry a child far more than the surrounding deadly events.

These people are searching among potato peelings for anything they can eat. Many died from starvation or cold during the Siege of Leningrad.

Try getting dressed in a hurry when they wake you every few hours of the night. You're only nine years old and you could sleep through any bomb raid or **artillery** barrage.

Your mother is rushing you: 'Quickly! Quickly!' But your boots have so many eyelets, it takes an interminable time to lace them up – no, that's not right, that's the wrong hole. But it's good enough. You pull on the second boot without bothering. You grab your bundle – that's it, off you go.

The air-raid shelter is in the neighbouring house. The road is dark. You know it well, but it's pockmarked with shell holes and your right foot gets caught in something, makes you stumble.

You search for the light – there it is! The shelter is well lit inside. There's still room to sit down. There are benches in the centre, at the entrance.

We waste no time in taking our places and piling up our bundles. There is already a rumbling sound in the far distance. They are firing, the bombs are dropping.

But it's not them I'm afraid of. I am hiding my right foot from the other people. I've just noticed that I'm wearing my grandmother's boot, laced up by one eyelet. Has no one seen it yet? I am so clumsy. It's five sizes too big. How could I have not seen that, even half asleep? How careless, what a muddlehead I am.

21

Fighting in the Philippines

The United States was confident that its powerful military presence in the Philippines would fend off any Japanese attacks. This island group, which lies south of Japan, had become a US possession in 1898 but by the 1930s was on its way to independence. The United States hoped to use it as a base to launch attacks on Japan.

Japanese troops attacked the Philippines in December 1941 and captured the capital, Manila, on 2 January 1942. A combined **Filipino**-US force, under US General Douglas MacArthur, fought hard but was defeated on the Bataan peninsula near Manila (9 April). After a month-long defence of the island of Corregidor (in Manila Bay) the Americans surrendered in May 1942. MacArthur vowed 'I shall return' – which he did, but only after a gap of two and a half years.

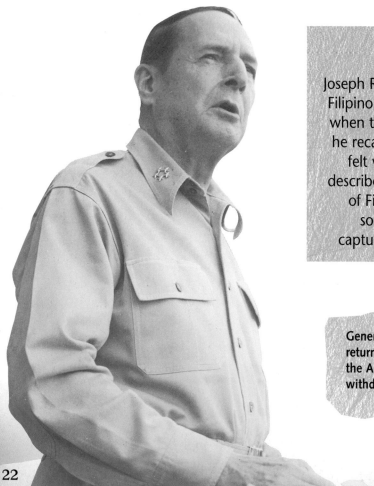

Joseph Romero's memories

Joseph Romero was a young Filipino boy living in Manila when the war started. Here he recalls the shock people felt when Bataan fell. He describes the 'death march' of Filipino and American soldiers who had been captured by the Japanese.

General MacArthur vowed to return to the Philippines after the Americans were forced to withdraw from there.

Starving and exhausted American and Filipino prisoners of war were forced to march across the Philippines. As many as 7000–10,000 died on what is known as the Bataan Death March.

Then, the impossible happened. Bataan fell and the march began. Stories preceded the prisoners' arrival in our town. The women of the town made small loaves of bread when they learned our soldiers were starving. We kids were designated to bring the bread and, more importantly, water to the soldiers. Then the soldiers started to arrive. They looked like skeletons. Americans are much taller than Filipinos and I thought you would die before you got as thin as they were. We brought the victuals to them. The Japanese were displeased to put it mildly. Fortunately they only hit us with their rifle butts to fend us off.

Guys were dying every day in the camp. We were close enough to see the burial details bring out the bodies. They would remove the deceased's clothes and shoes because the living needed them. The body was wrapped in paper and buried outside the barbed wire fence. Now and then, we would hear shots. These were executions.

The very last truck carrying prisoners finally turned off our **macadamized** road to the Death Camp. The prisoners threw their money into the air for us to grab. I didn't get any. I read a lie later that the people gave or sold food to the soldiers. The latter did not happen. When you consider the danger we were in there was no way we could bargain with the soldiers even if we were inclined to do so.

The enemy below

During the first years of the war, Germany's control of much of Europe meant the supply of essential goods to Great Britain became limited. The British relied on goods produced in parts of its empire (including Canada, South Africa and India) as well as a huge amount of products from the United States. Hitler hoped to starve the British into surrender, so it was vital to maintain sea routes in and out of the country in order to survive. Great Britain relied on cargo ships to carry food, building materials and fuel. The Battle of the Atlantic, intensifying in June 1940, saw German U-boats (submarines) patrolling sea lanes, trying to sink British ships with their **torpedoes**. British naval vessels tried to hunt down and destroy these U-boats.

The only way to protect ships was to send them in groups known as **convoys**, guarded by warships to try to ensure the safe passage of cargo. These convoys became even more important once the United States entered the war, as the ships carried thousands of US soldiers to war. Some of the most dangerous waters lay just west of Ireland, which remained neutral during the war. Villagers along Ireland's western coast often woke to find cargo – and bodies – washed up along the sands.

A British merchant ship sinking after being torpedoed by a German U-boat. Germany hoped to stop the supply of goods to Britain.

Brid MacDonncada's account

Brid MacDonncada, who was nineteen years old when the war began, lived on a small island off the west coast of Ireland. Three of her brothers had joined the war effort as American soldiers, so Brid needed to help her elderly parents look after their small farm. Here she tells the author of her experiences.

Cargo and sometimes bodies were washed ashore in the bays of western Ireland.

Although we were neutral, we relied on Britain for many of our goods. From the beginning of the war many items, such as flour, sugar and tobacco, were **rationed**. Shortages of meat and vegetables hurt people in Dublin, Galway and other big towns, but we were able to catch fish, grow potatoes and other crops, and to get enough dairy goods from our farm animals. Even sugar wasn't a concern, once people began relying on sugar beets rather than cane sugar. A big problem, though, was rubber. Everyone rode bicycles and soon it became impossible to get new tyres.

Things would wash up on the beach near us and by 1942 it was common to find something on the sand. We had to report some items, like rubber or barrels of oil, to the **civic guards** but the simple rule was that the cargo belonged to the person on whose beach it finished. Bodies also had to be reported. Fishermen found two bodies on Saint MacDara's Island, about three miles offshore. The bodies had no identification, so we buried them above the high-water mark. My cousins on the Aran Islands found the body of a young Scottish lad – he did have identification. He was buried in the church graveyard and local people tended his grave. His parents came over after the war and were so touched by the well-tended grave that they chose to let him stay there.

Women at war

World War II created enormous social changes. Before the war, men had most of the jobs and women remained at home as housewives. But with so many men called to join the armed services in Great Britain, the United States and other countries, women needed to carry on with the jobs that had once been seen as 'men's work'.

Apart from producing the normal goods that a country needs in peacetime – such as foods, clothing, cars, building materials and so on – the women needed to help with the 'war effort'. Some women volunteered to be nurses or to serve in special women's units of the army, navy and air force. Others remained as **civilians**, producing weapons and military equipment that could be used in battle, or helping to raise funds for the war. 'Rosie the Riveter', a fictional female labourer, became the symbol of all American women engaged in war-related work. Women often enjoyed their work experience and gained self-confidence, so that after the war many women kept full-time jobs.

Other groups of people, previously denied work opportunities, helped the Allied cause. African-Americans, Hispanics, Asians and other **minorities** played an important part in the war effort. Their contribution helped the cause of increased **civil rights** in the following decades.

Doreen Lingard's experience

Doreen Lingard was in her late teens when she joined the Women's Land Army, a British group that put women to work in the countryside. Here she recalls her time felling trees to produce lumber that would help tanks drive across loose sand.

Many women who went to work in industries to aid the war effort chose to continue working after the war.

We spent a lot of time felling birch in Lifton, just outside Exeter. You don't really have to be that strong for felling. It was a knack, like sawing. We had four-and-a-half-pound and six-pound axes. We preferred the six-pound ones. You got on faster with them. The hillside at Lifton was so steep you had to kneel on one knee to get the trees down. And we weren't allowed to leave a stump of more than four inches. There was a railway at the bottom of the hill. Before we started we had to build a wooden support to keep the timber from getting on to the line. As we felled the trees we would roll them down the hill so that they were stacked up against the support.

Every Sunday we had a special train. There were about twenty of us. We had to load the whole lot into the goods wagon and take it along the line towards Bridestowe. We were supposed to ride on the wagons, four on each corner, but we used to invade the engine cabin and blow the whistle all the way to Bridestowe. The locals complained about the noise we made but we didn't care. We used to blow it the next week just the same.

Members of the Women's Land Army were an important part of the war effort – they raised the crops that fed the troops.

War in the Pacific

Japan's advance across Asia was rapid and by early 1942 the Japanese controlled most of the East Asian mainland. The next step was to press southwards towards Australia, but they suffered their first real defeats in the Pacific to the east. The United States gained important naval victories at the Battles of the Coral Sea (May 1942) and Midway (June 1942). This allowed American troopships to move soldiers across the Pacific (see map on page 14).

The United States began a strategy of 'island-hopping' westwards. Japan itself was the eventual target, but along the way American forces had to capture Japanese-held islands one by one ('hopping' from one island to the next). This strategy was going to be difficult because the Japanese believed in fighting to the death.

Some of the worst fighting took place in the Solomon Islands in the south-western Pacific. On 7 August 1942, US Marines landed on Guadalcanal (the largest of the Solomons) in the first major attack on Japanese-held positions in the Pacific. After six months of fierce jungle fighting the Japanese were defeated, and the stage was set for further US victories.

US marines land on the island of Guadalcanal. They battled for six months in dense jungle where snakes, scorpions and diseases, such as malaria, were constant dangers.

Patrick Connolly's letter

Corporal Patrick ('Parky') Connolly [of Norwood, Massachusetts] was among the first US Marines to land on Guadalcanal on 7 August 1942. This letter to his mother was written soon after landing. He later developed malaria.

A fellow US Marine took this photo of Corporal Connolly just days after the landing.

Dear Ma

I don't know when or if you'll get this letter but I wanted to reassure you that I'm okay. I suppose when you read these words none of the message will be top secret any longer but I've got to be careful what I say. Otherwise the **censor** will cut holes in this until there's nothing left.

Landing craft got us from the ships to the shore of this palm-fringed island. In normal times it must be a tropical paradise, but what we faced looked more like a vision of hell. We were pinned down on the beach with machine-gun fire raking our positions and shells from our ships pounding the Japs ahead of us in the forest. We were still pretty much in that position as night fell. By then our ships were trading shots with some Japanese vessels offshore. The **tracers** going back and forth reminded me of a ghostly tennis match.

I guess the **bombardment** did the trick because we managed to fight our way through the Japanese positions. The fighting was bad enough but now some of the guys are facing another enemy: malaria. It gives you the creeps seeing well-built guys shivering in the jungle heat, but that's what it does to you. The officers are trying to increase the stores of **quinine**. So far I feel all right, though.

Take care

Son Parky

Defending Australia

Japan had made the same rapid progress through Asia as Germany had in Europe. Sweeping south and west, it had gained control of nearly all of East Asia. Although the United States may have halted Japan's progress to the east, there was a greater target to the south – Australia. In 1942 the Japanese began preparing for a major invasion of Australia and landed on the large island of New Guinea (just north of Australia; see map on page 14). That same year they began bombing northern Australia. The port of Darwin was a particular target.

Australia would have been an extremely important prize for the Japanese. It had long coastlines, with excellent harbours, facing the Pacific and Indian oceans as well as the South China Sea. Controlling Australia would cut off an important supply route from Europe and southern Africa to the Pacific. It would also strike a major blow against the US effort to sweep across the Pacific towards Japan. Australia was an important centre for repairing American ships and aircraft, and its modern hospitals provided treatment for troops recovering from wounds or disease.

More than anything else, though, the Japanese assault on Darwin was a challenge to Australian pride. The Australians responded by sending troops north to take on the Japanese in the mountainous countryside of New Guinea. Apart from the fierce resistance of the Japanese soldiers, the Australian troops faced two natural obstacles. The first was the thick jungle that made any progress difficult and often led to hand-to-hand combat on meeting the Japanese. The second was the danger of developing malaria, a deadly fever that thrives in such a hot, steamy climate. American forces eventually joined them from the north-east, but it took two long years to prevent the Japanese invasion.

Len Hill's memories

Len Hill was a member of the 22nd Australian Infantry Battalion, which saw action in New Guinea from 1943 to 1945. He was interviewed at home in Melbourne in 2001 about his experiences of fighting in the New Guinea highlands.

Australian soldiers carry a wounded man to find medical help.

Q. Did you have any idea what the **terrain** or climate was like [in New Guinea]?

A. No, not very much at all but we were awfully surprised when we did get to New Guinea. It was very mountainous, dense jungle, terrific rainfalls, terrific humidity, completely different world to the world we had lived in.

Q. Was there a lot of mud?

A. Oh yes! You would be up to your ankles in mud and sometimes almost up to your knees in mud and for an infantry man who slept outdoors and lived in the outdoors it was not very pleasant, but you became very accustomed to it and made the best of it and looked upon it as normal.

Q. Did many men suffer from malaria?

A. Yes. In different parts malaria was very bad, at one stage we and other units had 40% wastage with malaria, so that meant our strength was down.

Q. How was general **hygiene**? Did you get to bathe and wash very often?

A. If you were in action you did not have very much time to wash. If you were not in action of course you washed every day, there was water around. We would get water off our tent and very often there would be a sea, river or creek nearby. So water was not hard to get and hygiene was very important. If hygiene was poor there was tremendous illness.

Advancing through Italy

By 1943, the **Allies** were ready to take on the Germans in western Europe. The Soviet Union was successfully fending off German advances in the east, but its people were exhausted by the war. They were desperate for a 'second front' far from the Soviet Union where others could fight the Germans. The extra front would split the German forces and weaken their presence in the Soviet Union.

Allied soldiers made their first real assault on western Europe after landing in southern Italy in July 1943 and slowly working their way northwards. After the fall of Benito Mussolini and Italy's surrender that same year, the Germans took over the fighting. They defended Italy fiercely, as whoever controlled Italy had a great advantage in the war in Europe. The advancing Allies were aided considerably by the efforts of the **partisans**, Italians who had never supported Mussolini or the Germans.

The Germans had powerful defences just south of Rome, so the Allies decided to avoid them by landing forces on Italy's west coast. They chose Anzio for the attack on 22 January 1944. Even this new assault, however, failed to shake the stiff German defence. The Allies would use the lessons of this hard-fought campaign later that year, when they mounted a more dramatic attack on western France.

The ruins of the monastery at Monte Cassino (inland from Anzio) in 1944, after months of attack by Allied troops.

Milton Briggs' account

Milton Briggs was a radio man aboard the light battle cruiser USS *Brooklyn*, which shelled German defensive positions during the Anzio landing. His account shows the vivid reactions of men exposed to terrible dangers.

How can I describe Anzio? How can a man describe Hell? I spent from Jan. 22, 1944 until June 6, 1944 in that inferno. On just one night all that was a boy in me died. On that night, I died in every way except in body. Hell should hold no fear for me because I was in Hell for four hours and lived to remember it.

We were called by the besieged Army to assist on one more bombardment run. We entered the battle run at 7:45 pm and were trapped by bombers. The run normally took 45 minutes, [but] we were unable to manoeuvre. In the next four hours, our destroyer was **torpedoed**. To my right the British cruiser *Penelope* was sunk. To my left, the British cruiser *Spartan* went down. We held our breath, prayed and waited for an end that didn't come. Ahead, a hospital ship was burning. All day they had been loading her with wounded. How many died, only God could tell. Another hospital ship steamed seaward, her hull cherry red from her flames.

The **beachhead** was in flames and the sky was alight with fire and smoke. The scene numbed us on the bridge as we lay there, and our tongues were silent as death. One ensign, on his knees, gave out with 'God save us!' and I guess God answered. In the brilliance of the flares, the faces were so white with fear that still in memory, 40 years later, I still see the goose bumps standing up, each with its hair in the center.

D-Day

The biggest military operation of the war came on 6 June 1944, when 150,000 British, Canadian and American soldiers were transported across the English Channel from England to Normandy in German-held France. This was the long-awaited 'second front', which would begin the difficult job of driving the Germans back from their conquered lands in western Europe.

The attack became known as 'D-Day' because the exact date ('D') was kept secret until the last minute. In fact, bad weather had delayed it by two days. Despite the delay, the D-Day operation had an element of surprise since the Germans had expected an attack further north, near the port of Calais. The French coastline was still heavily defended, however, with powerful **artillery** and machine-gun nests prepared to fire at anyone who arrived by sea.

On 6 June 1944 Allied forces land on five beaches on the Normandy coast. From these points the German troops are gradually driven out from their conquered lands in western Europe.

After heavy losses on both sides, the **Allies** secured their **beachheads** and within weeks controlled all of the Cotentin peninsula in Normandy. After two months of heavy fighting they began pushing the Germans back from the mainland. They then made progress eastward through France. For many people on both sides of the war, the end was now in sight.

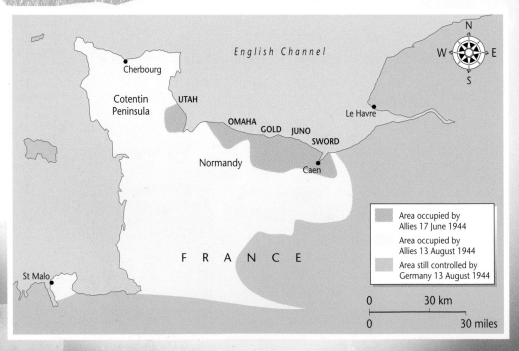

English Channel

Cherbourg

Cotentin Peninsula

UTAH

OMAHA

GOLD JUNO

SWORD

Le Havre

Normandy

Caen

F R A N C E

St Malo

N
W E
S

Area occupied by Allies 17 June 1944

Area occupied by Allies 13 August 1944

Area still controlled by Germany 13 August 1944

0   30 km

0   30 miles

Jim Wilkins' experience

Jim Wilkins of The Queen's Own Rifles of Canada spent much of 1943 and early 1944 at sea, getting used to the landing craft that would take Allied soldiers to the French beaches. Here he describes how he was severely wounded during the landing.

The ramp goes down and without hesitation my section leader, Cpl. John Gibson, jumps out well over his waist in water. He only makes a few yards and is killed. We have landed dead on into a **pillbox** with a machine gun blazing away at us. We didn't hesitate and jumped into the water one after the other – I was last of the first row. Tommy Dalrymple and Kenny Scott are just in front of me when something hits my left **magazine** pouch and stops me up short for a moment. The round had gone right through two magazines, entered my left side and came out my back. Kenny keeps yelling, 'Come on, come on' – 'I'm coming, I'm coming' I yell to him.

We are now up to our knees in water and you can hear a kind of buzzing sound all around as well as the sound of the machine gun itself. All of a sudden something slapped the side of my right leg and then a round caught me dead centre up high on my right leg causing a compound fracture. By this time I was flat on my face in the water – I've lost my rifle, my helmet is gone and Kenny is still yelling at me to come on. He is also shot in the upper leg but has no broken bones. I yell back, 'I can't, my leg is broken'. I flop over onto my back and start to float to shore where I meet five other riflemen all in very bad shape. The man beside me is dead within minutes.

American assault soldiers disembarking from their landing craft at a beachhead on D-Day.

Air raids on Germany

Germany would not be defeated easily with just a land-based attack, no matter how large. British and American commanders agreed that they needed to mount a long **campaign** of bombing raids on German cities before – and after – **Allied** troops landed in France. They would target industrial cities which supplied arms and equipment for the Nazi war machine.

By mid 1943 these bombing raids were under way, with American bombers making raids during daylight and British planes taking over at night. Many men and aircraft were lost during these dangerous raids, especially the daylight runs when German **anti-aircraft** guns could target the bombers. The effect on the Germans was also terrible, with many major cities reduced to rubble and hundreds of thousands of people killed or made homeless. The raids did have their intended effect, as Germany found it almost impossible to produce enough goods to defend itself. Also with Nazi troops and equipment moved to defend German cities, the Allies found it easier to push eastward through France.

A RAF Halifax bomber makes a night bombing raid over Germany.

Heinrich Kloppenburg's description

Heinrich Kloppenburg was at home in his flat when Allied planes bombed his native Bremerhaven on 18 September 1944. His recollections recall the words of Colin Parry (see pages 12–13) during London's **Blitz** four years earlier.

In the meantime, the hollow sound of the anti-aircraft **artillery** had turned into a raging one, an indication that the squadron was attacking at low altitude. Indeed, one could hear from the basement entry airplanes fly close by over us, with an eerily howling noise. Not only that, almost simultaneously one sensed a close sequence of peculiarly clicking sounds, obviously caused by stick-type **incendiary** bombs, which broke through the roofs of our own and the neighbouring houses.

Before we realized what had happened, the ground trembled again and the electric lights went out. Has the house been hit over our heads? All energies of hell seemed to descend on us, with horrible howling, cracking and trembling the hour of the **apocalypse** seemed to come. Here, underground, surrounded by darkness we stood, helpless, bewildered, unable to comprehend what happened around us.

I had a small rechargeable torch with me. Utilizing it, I hurried to fetch the lantern for emergencies, hanging in the **antechamber**, and I lit it, not without noticing that my hands attempting to light the wick with a match were trembling considerably. The lamp soon spread steady light, and this, together with the soothing words of the men, contributed to preventing the spread of panic.

The Battle of the Bulge

The **Allies**, after the successful D-Day landings, swept across France but then became stalled at the German border in late 1944. Bad weather kept their aircraft grounded, so the Germans launched a **counter-attack** northward into Belgium and Luxembourg in December 1944. The Germans were becoming desperate, and supplies were running very low. Only a dramatic victory here could prevent their eventual defeat. They aimed to divide the Allies and regain control of Antwerp and other important cities in northern Europe. At first, the Germans seemed to succeed, as they created a 'bulge' in the Allied lines.

Cold, rainy weather and the thickly wooded **terrain** made it hard for the Allies to use tanks and other heavy equipment, but still they stood up to this advance. After terrible fighting in bad conditions, they pushed back the 'bulge' and drove the enemy into its own territory. The war in Europe would continue for four more months, but the Allied success here ended any German hope of ultimate victory.

A soldier patrols a deserted town during the Battle of the Bulge.

Extract from a history of the US 80th Infantry Division
This extract comes from a history of the US 80th Infantry Division, which was in the thick of the fighting during the Battle of the Bulge. It describes how US forces drove into Germany after withstanding the first attack.

Thunder of **artillery** occasionally broke the stillness of the murky night. Suddenly at 0200 Feb. 7, 1945, the entire front burst into flame. Artillery shells screamed towards Germany's 'sacred soil' in a **crescendo**, drowning out the maddening **din** of men going into action.

The battle-tested 80th 'Blue Ridge' Division again was moving forward, having helped smash the flank of Field Marshal von Rundstedt's Luxembourg **salient**. ...To reach the Nazi fortifications, the Our and Sauer rivers had to be hurdled. Constant rains, melting snow from surrounding hills had transformed them into raging torrents.

War correspondent Gene Currivan described the action as follows:
'The boys trudged doggedly through the woods and down a steep slope to the river. It was a rugged crossing ahead... Long before they reached the river they fell on their faces a dozen times as **screaming meemies** tore through the magnificent **coniferous** forest over their heads...

The river was swollen ten feet above its normal level and the current was so swift that many empty assault boats were swamped on the return trip. Machine gun fire and artillery fire from over the hill made the operation difficult, but by the aid of a smoke screen which made the river disappear in a dense fog, the assault craft managed to get across carrying the boys into Germany.

HOSPITAL PLANT 44..

APO .... c/o POSTMASTER

DEAR Mrs. Barbara Connolly

I am pleased to inform you that on 25 FEB 1945 (Date) your

Son Pvt James P. Connolly, 31422356 (Grade, name, Army serial number)
(Relationship)

was MAKING NORMAL IMPROVEMENT

Diagnosis† Frostbite of feet. Very truly yours,

* Enter present status as—
  Making normal improvement.
  Convalescing.
† Must be written in nontechnical language.

PAUL N SIEGEL
1st. Lt. Med. Adm. C.

W. D., A. G. O. Form 234
9 November 1944

The author's father suffered frostbite in the freezing conditions of the Battle of the Bulge. Relatives feared receiving cards like these, in case the news was even worse.

The Holocaust

One of the most horrifying elements of **Nazi** Germany was the belief that Germans were a 'master race' and that other nationalities were **inferior**. Taking this idea further, Adolf Hitler and his government – even before the war – made Jewish people the particular target of their hatred. Many German Jews fled their country before the war, forced out by anti-Jewish laws and violence against their **synagogues**, property and themselves.

Conditions for European Jews got even worse once the war began. As Nazi forces conquered much of Europe, millions of Jews – along with **communists**, homosexuals, gypsies and other 'inferior' people – were rounded up and imprisoned in **concentration camps**. There they were forced to work like slaves, causing many of the old and weak to fall ill and die. Many more were brutally killed in concentration camp gas chambers.

By the end of the war, the Nazis had killed nearly six million Jewish men, women and children. We use the term **Holocaust** (from Greek words meaning 'whole' and 'burnt') to describe this terrible chapter in World War II.

> 'By means of shrewd lies, unremittingly repeated, it is possible to make people believe that heaven is hell – and hell heaven. The greater the lie, the more readily it will be believed.'
> (Adolf Hitler, *Mein Kampf*)

Judith Jagermann's memories

Judith Jagermann (born Judith Pinczovsky) was a nine-year-old Jewish girl living in Czechoslovakia when the war began. Life for Czech Jews became very difficult after Germany occupied Czechoslovakia in 1939. In 1941, the Pinczovsky family (Judith, her parents and her sister Ruth) were sent to the Auschwitz concentration camp. Here she describes life in Birkenau, the section of Auschwitz where the Pinczovsky women were sent. Judith, her mother and Ruth survived and settled in Israel after the war. Her father died in Auschwitz.

The roll calls in Birkenau were horrible. They drove us already at half past four in the morning from the barracks and would let us stand for hours at a time at attention, either in the freezing cold or during a heatwave. Many women could not take it and fainted, being already extremely weak due to the lack of food, while the cold also bothered us a lot. My feet were totally frostbitten. I had only wooden house-shoes which were constantly falling off my feet, because Birkenau had, during winter, heavy mud in which my house-shoes got stuck.

Children look out from behind the barbed wire fence at the Nazi concentration camp in Auschwitz. Many people were killed there, or did not survive the cruel conditions.

Mama had torn her blanket apart and had made bands to swathe my legs to keep them a little warmer. But my legs became worse all the time; it was terribly cold, -20°C, (i.e. 20 degrees Centigrade below zero) and the frostbites became open wounds, infected with puss.

The daily roll calls which took hours, were totally senseless. Occasionally 2-3 times daily and only in order to annoy us. More and more people collapsed. They just were shot and taken away. The eternal barbed wire was our only view and all the camps were divided by high tension wires. Many people committed suicide in this way; they simply would crawl up to the barbed wires and would die immediately, glued to the wires.

Through Burma

The final phase of the land war in Asia was concentrated in the steamy jungles and highlands of Burma. The Japanese, who had conquered Burma in 1942, were trying to prevent **Allied** forces from restoring important rail and road connections, so that supplies and equipment could not get through to China (see map on page 14). The restored link with China would be a powerful boost for the Allies' war effort. It would mean that Japan would be almost surrounded.

By early 1945 the Allies had already begun two major pushes from other directions. Troops from Australia, New Zealand and the United States were pushing northward through New Guinea (see pages 30–31). At the same time, US forces were pushing westward across the Pacific towards Japan. By March 1945 they were close enough to mount regular bombing raids against Japan itself. These raids established a pattern of airborne attack that would eventually enable the Americans to use the atomic bomb on Japan.

At about the same time, with Germany nearly defeated, the British could now send many more troops to fight in this important Asian region. British, Indian and Gurkha (Nepalese) troops joined American forces to make their way slowly through the dense **terrain**.

Over the space of four months, the Allied forces retook river ports and railways that had been under Japanese control for more than three years, but the Japanese resisted stubbornly, knowing that this was their last chance to keep control of Southeast Asia. Fighting was fierce and often hand-to-hand combat. As with fighting in New Guinea (see pages 30–31), the soldiers had to deal with malaria and other tropical illnesses. By May 1945 the Japanese had been driven out of Burma.

Lance Corporal Masao Kojima's description
Lance Corporal Masao Kojima of the Japanese Army describes the fighting conditions in late May 1945, as British troops were completing their advance through Burma.

British soldiers on the look out for enemy troops. Fighting in the dense jungle of Burma often meant hand-to-hand combat.

We were broken through by British tanks at Pynmana and Toungoo, and we were ordered to retreat to Moulmein via a mountain route between the Sittang and Salwen Rivers. We marched along a good road to Mawchi. There we were told that we had to walk over rugged mountain paths to Papun, our next supply point. After only a day's rest we climbed the mountains on 30 May 1945 carrying the heavy load of fifteen days' rations on our shoulders. It rained every day, beginning the notorious rainy season, and our going was extremely hard, slipping and sinking in mud. Our 7th Company had been allocated six oxen for carrying rations and ammunition, but their legs sank deep in the mud and soldiers had to pull them out which was exhausting. I walked at the tail end of the company, encouraging tired soldiers to go on. An elderly private, an assistant medic, was really exhausted and almost dropped out. I let him throw everything away, medicine bag, rifle, bayonet and **duffel bag**, except one grenade (for suicide), and hit his hip with a bamboo stick saying: 'A little further to go. Stand up and advance. It will be the end of your life if you do not keep up with us.'
'I don't mind dying here. Let me stay here as I cannot walk any more.'
'Remember, you have a wife and children. Do you want to be a white skeleton left in the wild mountains?'
'It's my body. Leave it alone. You hit me with a bamboo.'
'If you are angry for being beaten, stay alive!'

Yalta

By early 1945 it was apparent to the **Allied** leaders that victory was in sight. The question was: what should happen to Europe, and to Germany especially, after the war ended? The leaders of the 'Big Three' countries (British Prime Minister Winston Churchill, Soviet Premier Joseph Stalin and US President Franklin Roosevelt) met in the Soviet coastal resort of Yalta in February 1945. There they discussed ways to prevent Germany from ever conducting a similar war. They decided to divide up Germany, with a different Allied country supervising each German zone.

The talks showed that some of the differences between the Big Three themselves, which had been put aside during the war, could become problems in the years to come. Although they were allies, the leaders were wary of each other. Roosevelt did not approve of a continued British Empire, while Churchill feared the **economic** strength that the United States could use to gain power after the war. Stalin worried that the other two leaders would turn on his country because of their dislike of **communism**. Despite these differences – and maybe because of them – the leaders focused on ways to preserve peace throughout the world. The discussions also paved the way for the creation of the United Nations, a world peacekeeping organization.

From left to right, Winston Churchill, Franklin Roosevelt and Joseph Stalin meet at Yalta to discuss the peace and how to prevent another war.

An exchange between Winston Churchill and Joseph Stalin
This exchange shows how the Soviet leader angrily believed that the British (and possibly the United States) feared and distrusted his country. Winston Churchill, however, tries to keep the subject on world peace.

Winston Churchill: The peace of the world depends upon the lasting friendship of the three great powers, but His Majesty's Government feel we should be putting ourselves in a false position if we put ourselves in the position of trying to rule the world when our desire is to serve the world and preserve it from a renewal of the frightful horrors which have fallen upon the mass of its inhabitants...

Joseph Stalin: ...I would like to ask Mr. Churchill to name the power which may intend to dominate the world. I am sure Great Britain does not want to dominate the world. So one is removed from suspicion. I am sure the United States does not wish to do so, so another is excluded from the powers having intentions to dominate the world.

Winston Churchill: I know that under the leaders of the three powers as represented here we may feel safe. But these leaders may not live for ever. In ten years' time we may disappear. A new generation will come which did not experience the horrors of war and may probably forget what we have gone through. We would like to secure the peace for at least fifty years. We have now to build up such a status, such a plan, that we can put as many obstacles as possible to the coming generation quarrelling among themselves.

V-E Day

By the spring of 1945 the **Allies** had begun to close in on Germany to finish the war. British troops moved northward through Italy while US forces (from western Europe) and Soviet forces (from the east) swept through Germany. The Soviets surrounded Germany's capital, Berlin. Hitler knew the end was in sight, and on 30 April he committed suicide in Berlin. Hitler's successor, Grand Admiral Karl Dönitz, sent a representative to sign an unconditional surrender on 7 May 1945.

The war against the **Nazis** and their European allies ended on 8 May 1945, following Germany's surrender. Although Japan was still at war, there was great rejoicing around the world. Families looked forward to being reunited with soldiers and sailors who had been away from home for many years.

That date, known as V-E Day (Victory in Europe Day), saw millions of people take to the streets in celebrations. The war in Europe was finally over.

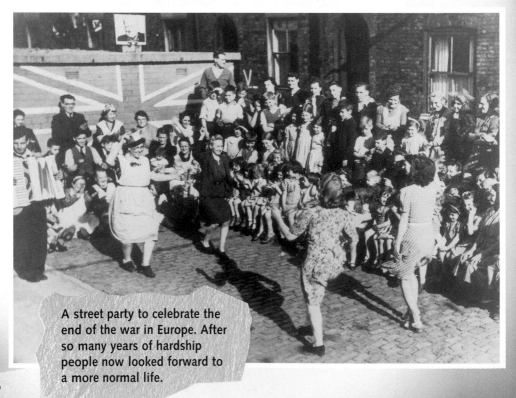

A street party to celebrate the end of the war in Europe. After so many years of hardship people now looked forward to a more normal life.

A report from the *Hereford Times*
On the evening of V-E Day thousands of bonfires were lit across Britain. At the top were **effigies** of Hitler and his fellow Nazis. In this extract a reporter for the *Hereford Times* describes the bonfire in the little village of Stoke Lacy.

Passing through the village of Stoke Lacy early on Tuesday afternoon one was startled to see an effigy of Hitler in the car park at the Plough. That evening a crowd began to gather, and word went around that Hitler was to be consumed in flames at 11 pm. At that hour excitement was intense, when Mr W. R. Symonds called upon Mr S. J. Parker, the commander of No 12 Platoon of the **Home Guard**, to set the effigy alight. In a few minutes the body of Hitler disintegrated as his 1000 years' empire had done. First his arm, poised in the Hitler salute, dropped as smartly as it was ever raised in life... Then a leg fell off, and the flames burnt fiercely to the strains of 'Rule Britannia', 'There'll Always be an England' and 'Roll Out the Barrel'. Then the crowd spontaneously linked hands and in a circle 300 strong sang 'Auld Lang Syne'. Mr Parker then called for three cheers for Mr Churchill, President Truman, Marshal Stalin and our serving boys and girls. The ceremony was followed by the singing of 'God Save the King'.

Crowds celebrate V-E day (8 May 1945) in New York.

The atomic bomb

Germany surrendered on 7 May 1945 – but the war was not over. As it became clear that Japan was going to fight on, with the loss of many lives on both sides, the US began to discuss with the **Allies** the possibility of using a new bomb they had developed: the atomic bomb.

On 16 July 1945 an atomic bomb was tested in the New Mexico desert. It produced a huge blast of energy. The tower the bomb was fixed to vanished completely, and the sand directly around it was heated so much that it turned to glass. US President Truman decided to use the new weapon on the Japanese city of Hiroshima on 6 August 1945. Three days later, another bomb was dropped on the city of Nagasaki. Emperor Hirohito told his political leaders to surrender on 14 August 1945. The final surrender document was signed on 2 September 1945.

The scientists who produced the atomic bomb understood that it could cause a huge amount of damage. However, neither they nor the people who decided to drop the bombs fully understood the far-reaching damage that would be caused by the **radiation** released when the bomb exploded. We can also imagine the confusion it caused – no one in Japan even knew that such a powerful weapon existed until it was used.

It is estimated that 140,000 people were killed as a result of the bomb dropped on Hiroshima. This building was directly under the blast. It survived and has been preserved to remember those who died and to remind people of the horrifying power of atomic weapons.

Akira Onogi's experience

Akira Onogi was sixteen years old when the bomb was dropped on Hiroshima. He was at home, 1.2 km (about three quarters of a mile) away from the centre of the explosion. The house was under the shade of a warehouse, which protected him from the first blast.

MR ONOGI: I was reading lying on the floor, then I saw a blue flash of light just like a spark made by a train or some short circuit. Next, a steam-like blast came.

INTERVIEWER: From which direction?

MR ONOGI: Well, I'm not sure, anyway, when the blast came, my friend and I were blown into another room. I was unconscious for a while, and when I came to, I found myself in the dark. Thinking my house was directly hit by a bomb, I removed red soil and roof tiles covering me by hand and for the first time I saw the sky. I found that all the houses around there had collapsed for as far as I could see.

INTERVIEWER: All the houses?

MR ONOGI: Yes, well, I couldn't see anyone around me but I heard somebody shouting, 'Help! Help!' from somewhere. Then, I looked next door and I saw the father of the neighbouring family standing almost naked. His skin was peeling off all over his body and was hanging from [his] fingertips. I talked to him but he was too exhausted to give me a reply.

'It was not clear to me that our course was unjustified. Even now I am not sure how future historians will allocate the responsibility for the war.'
(Japanese Emperor Hirohito to US General Douglas MacArthur in the days after Japan's surrender.)

What have we learnt from World War II?

There is no doubt that World War II was the largest, costliest and deadliest war in history. Sixty-one countries, representing three-quarters of the world's population, took part and more than 110 million people were actively involved. The human cost was terrifying: 25 million military deaths and 35 million **civilian** deaths, as well as millions more who were wounded or made homeless. Many countries, even on the **Allied** side, found that their **economies** were almost destroyed by the war effort.

Previous wars had touched the lives of ordinary civillians, but as a rule most of the fighting took place well away from major population centres. World War II was different. From the very beginning, it became clear that anywhere – and anyone – in enemy territory was a possible target. Railways, roads, cities and towns were destroyed by **artillery** and air raids. Millions of people lost their lives as it became clear that there was nowhere to hide from the horrors of the war. One of the most tragic episodes in human history, the **Holocaust** (see pages 40–41), involved the deliberate killing of more than five million innocent people.

At the end of World War I, world leaders had tried to build a lasting peace. By forming the **League of Nations** they had hoped to turn World War I into 'the war to end all wars'. The League, however, was not strong enough to prevent a second world conflict. At the end of the second, even more brutal, conflict world leaders were even more determined to build a peaceful world.

Representatives from 50 nations met in San Francisco on 25 April 1945 to decide on a charter for a new organization, known as the United Nations. The charter was signed on 26 June; it became effective on 24 October 1945.

An extract from the UN Charter
This extract comes from the beginning of the UN Charter and it expresses the views of the representatives who sought to build a world based on co-operation and peace rather than rivalries and conflict.

UN soldiers check their weapon in Sarajevo, Bosnia in 1995. United Nations peacekeeping troops are sent to various parts of the world where fighting has broken out.

Charter of the United Nations
We the Peoples of the United Nations...
United for a Better World

WE THE PEOPLES OF THE UNITED NATIONS DETERMINED
- to save succeeding generations from the scourge of war, which twice in our lifetime has brought untold sorrow to mankind
- to reaffirm faith in fundamental human rights, in the dignity and worth of the human person, in the equal rights of men and women and of nations large and small
- to establish conditions under which justice and respect for the obligations arising from treaties and other sources of international law can be maintained
- to promote social progress and better standards of life in larger freedom

AND FOR THESE ENDS
- to practice tolerance and live together in peace with one another as good neighbours
- to unite our strength to maintain international peace and security
- to ensure, by the acceptance of principles and the institution of methods, that armed force shall not be used, save in the common interest
- to employ international machinery for the promotion of the economic and social advancement of all peoples

HAVE RESOLVED TO COMBINE OUR EFFORTS TO ACCOMPLISH
THESE AIMS
Accordingly, our respective Governments, through representatives assembled in the city of San Francisco, who have exhibited their full powers found to be in good and due form, have agreed to the present Charter of the United Nations and do hereby establish an international organization to be known as the United Nations.

Timeline

| 1939 | Sept 1 | **Nazis** invade Poland |
| | Sept 3 | Britain, France, Australia and New Zealand declare war on Germany |

1940	May 10	Nazis invade France, Belgium, Luxembourg and the Netherlands; Winston Churchill becomes British Prime Minister
	May 26	Evacuation of **Allied** troops from Dunkirk begins
	Jun 3	Germans bomb Paris
	Jul 10	Battle of Britain begins
	Aug 25/26	First British air raid on Berlin
	Sept 7	German **Blitz** against England begins

1941	May 10/11	Heavy German bombing of London; British bomb Hamburg
	Jun 22	Germany attacks Soviet Union as Operation Barbarossa begins
	Sept 8	Nazi **siege** of Leningrad begins
	Dec 7	Japanese bomb Pearl Harbor
	Dec 8	United States and Britain declare war on Japan
	Dec 11	Hitler declares war on United States

1942	In June	Mass murder of Jews by gassing begins at Auschwitz **concentration camp**
	Sept 13	Battle of Stalingrad begins
	Nov 1	'Operation Supercharge' Allies break **Axis** lines at El Alamein.

1943	Feb 2	Germans surrender at Stalingrad in the first big defeat of Hitler's armies
	May 13	German and Italian troops surrender in North Africa
	Jul 25/26	Mussolini arrested and **Fascist** government falls
	Sept 8	Italian surrender announced
	Oct 13	Italy declares war on Germany
	Nov 18	Large British air raid on Berlin

1944	Jan 22	Allies land at Anzio in Italy
	Jan 27	Leningrad relieved after 900-day siege
	Feb 16	Germans **counter-attack** against Anzio **beachhead**
	May 25	Germans retreat from Anzio
	Jun 6	D-Day landings
	Jul 25–30	Operation Cobra begins in Normandy; US troops break out west of St Lô
	Dec 16–27	Battle of the Bulge in the Ardennes

1945	Feb 4-11	Roosevelt, Churchill and Stalin meet at Yalta
	May 7	**Unconditional** surrender of all German forces to Allies
	May 8	VE (Victory in Europe) Day
	Aug 6	First atomic bomb dropped, on Hiroshima, Japan
	Aug 14	Japanese agree to unconditional surrender

Find out more

Books and websites

20th Century Perspectives: Key Battles of World War II, Fiona Reynoldson
(Heinemann Library, 2001)
Causes and Consequences of the Second World War, Stewart Ross (Evans Books, 1995)
The Blitz, Stewart Ross (Evans Books, 2001)

Go exploring! Log on to Heinemann's online history resource at
www.heinemannexplore.co.uk
www.spartacus.schoolnet.co.uk has information about all aspects of World War II
www.sptimes.ru/archive/sppress/91 is a Russian website (in English) of personal
experiences of the Russian people in World War II
www.localheroes.8m.com has interviews with Australians who fought in World War II

List of Primary Sources

The author and publisher gratefully acknowledge the following publications and
websites from which written sources in the book are drawn. In some cases the
wording or sentence structure have been simplified to make the material appropriate
for a school readership.

P. 9: General Rommel: www.ibiscom.com/blitzkrieg.htm
P 11: Hubert Banner: *We'll Meet Again: A Personal and Social History of World War Two,* Vera Lynn,
with Robin Cross and Jenny de Gex, (London: Sidgwick & Jackson, 1989)
P 13: Colin Perry: *Boy in the Blitz,* (Corgi 1974)
P 15: George Phraner: www.execpc.com/~dschaaf/phraner.html
P 17: *125 Years in Words and Pictures as Described in Contemporary Events in The Daily Telegraph
1855–1980*
P 19: Victor Bruce: www.dashmark.com.au/singapore/
P 21: Lyudmila Anopova: http://www.sptimes.ru/archive/sppress/91/siege.html
P 23: Joseph Romero: http:www.culturalbridge.com/phwwii6.htm
P 25: Brid Macdonncada (author's mother): told to the author
P 27: Doreen Lingard: *They Fought in the Fields The Women's Land Army: The Story of a Forgotten
Victory,* Nicola Tyrer, (Sinclair-Stevenson, 1996)
P 29: Patrick Connolly (author's uncle) letter in author's family's possession
P 31: Len Hill: www.localheroes.8m.com
P 33: Milton Briggs: http://home.nc.rr.com/alpanebianco
P 35: Jim Wilkins: http://users.erols.com/wolfy/qor/html/body_wilkins.html
P 37: Heinrich Kloppenburg: www.zum.de/psm/ns/kloppenburg2_e.php
P 39: 80th Infantry Division: from a document in the author's possession
P 41: Judith Jagermann: *If This is a Man* and *The Truce,* Primo Levi, Penguin Modern Classics
(Viking Press, 1979)
P 43: Masao Kojima: *Tales by Japanese Soldiers of the Burma Campaign 1942-1945,* John Nunneley and
Kazuo Tamayama. (Cassell, 2000).
P 45: Winston Churchill and Joseph Stalin: www.spartacus.schoolnet.co.uk/2WWyalta.htm
P 47: *Hereford Times* report from *We'll Meet Again: A Personal and Social History of World War Two,*
Vera Lynn, with Robin Cross and Jenny de Gex (Sidgwick & Jackson, 1989).
P 49: Akira Onogi: http://www.inicom.com/hibakusha/
P 51: Preamble from the United Nations Charter: http://www.un/org/aboutun/charter/

Glossary

aerial taking place in the air

aft (on ships) at or towards the rear

Allied referring to the countries, including Great Britain, France, the United States and the Soviet Union, which fought against the Axis powers

antechamber entrance to a larger room

anti-aircraft ground-based guns that are aimed at enemy aircraft

apocalypse widespread disaster

appeasement offering a warlike country (like Nazi Germany) some concessions in return for a promise not to go to war

artillery large guns

Axis describing the military forces of Germany, Italy, Japan and the countries that fought with them during World War II

beachhead coastal military position that has been reached by sea

bias judgement that is clouded by personal opinion

bivouac, bivouacked hurriedly prepared military camp

blitz, the Blitz sudden violent attack, especially from aircraft

bombardment prolonged attack by artillery or by bombing

campaign attack or series of attacks over a long period

causeway raised road or walkway connecting an island to the mainland

censor someone who removes sensitive military information from letters or newspaper reports during a war

charnel house place where the bodies or bones of the dead are placed

civic guards police or their representatives in Ireland

civil rights basic human rights that are guaranteed by law

civilian someone who is not directly involved in armed combat

communism political system where the state controls property, industry and trade

concentration camp military prison in which people are usually treated harshly. The Nazi government mainly used them to imprison millions of Jews. Many were murdered in special gas chambers.

coniferous evergreen

convoy group of ships or vehicles travelling together for protection

cordon roped-off area

correspondent reporter

counter-attack attack against an army or group that has just attacked

crescendo increasingly loud noise

demoralize wear down an enemy's will to fight back

din noise that is loud enough to be confusing

duffel bag large bag, carried over the shoulder, containing a soldier's belongings

economy overall system of work, payment, business etc within a country

effigy model, usually mocking, of a person

evacuation withdrawal from, or abandoning of a position

fascist type of government, usually headed by a dictator, believing in the superiority of its country and favouring strong military power. Any opposition to the government is usually brutally opposed.

Filipino native of the Philippines

fleet the overall collection of naval vessels in an area

fusillade series of shots or explosions at the same time

Holocaust   term used to describe the imprisonment and killing of millions of Jews by the Nazi government

Home Guard   volunteer military group that protected Britain during World War II

hygiene   overall standards of cleanliness

incendiary   designed to create fires

infamy   extremely bad or evil reputation

inferior   less important than

isolationism   unwillingness to take part in a war that does not seem to concern one's own country

League of Nations   international peacekeeping organization involving 63 countries, lasting from 1920 to 1946

macadamized   fully paved

magazine   place where ammunition is stored

minority   group that makes up less than half of a larger group, like African-Americans and Hispanics in the United States

Nazi   (short for 'National Socialist' in German), the ruling German political party during World War II

pandemonium   noise and confusion

partisan   someone who fought as a rebel against the governing military powers once his (or her) own country had been defeated

pillbox   concrete building containing machine guns and other weapons

primary source   original document or object from the past which helps us understand a historical event or era

propaganda   information that is published (and sometimes even changed) to sway public opinion

pyre   pile that is prepared for burning

quinine   naturally occurring substance that is used as a treatment for malaria

radar   electronic system of detecting aircraft, other aerial objects and ships

radiation   waves of energy which can cause long-term damage to people's health

rationed   distributed in small quantities because of short supply

salvo   group of bombs or artillery shells coming all at the same time

salient   hill or ridge that juts out from its surroundings, or a bulge in a battleline

scourge   person or thing that dishes out punishment or pain

screaming meemies   slang term for rockets that hummed and whistled while in flight

secondary source   account based upon the evidence of past events

siege   prolonged attack against a surrounded city or fort

synagogue   building where Jews worship

terrain   land, especially land on which fighting occurs

torpedo   long, tubular bomb sent underwater to destroy ships and submarines

tracer   bullets or artillery shells that leave a trail of light or sparks to help artillery soldiers aim

unconditional   with no conditions or exceptions, complete

Index

aerial combat 10–11
Allied powers 4, 5, 14, 16, 20, 32, 34, 36,
    38, 42, 44, 46, 50
appeasement policy 4
Atlantic, Battle of the 24
atomic bomb 42, 48–9
Australia 30–1, 42
Axis powers 4, 5, 16

Belguim 8, 38
Blitz 7, 12–13
blitzkrieg 8, 9
bombing raids 5, 19,12–13, 42, 36–7, 50
Britain 4, 10–13, 16, 18, 24, 26, 34, 36, 42,
    44
Britain, Battle of 10–11
British Empire 18, 44
Bulge, Battle of the 38–9
Burma 42–3

Canada 24, 34, 35
Churchill, Winston 10, 13, 18, 44, 45
civilian deaths 12, 20, 48, 50
concentration camps 40–1

D-Day 5, 34–5

Egypt 16
El Alamein, Battle of 16–17

fascism 4
France 4, 5, 8, 9, 34–5
Frank, Anne 7

Germany 4, 5, 8, 10, 12, 16, 20, 32, 36–7,
    38, 40, 44, 46
Guadalcanal 28

Hiroshima 48, 49
Hitler, Adolf 4, 10, 24, 40, 46, 47
Holocaust 40–1, 50

Ireland 24–5
isolationism 4, 14
Italy 4, 5, 32–3

Japan 4, 5, 14, 15, 18, 19, 22, 28, 30, 42–3,
    46, 48–9
Jewish people 40–1
jungle combat 28, 29, 30, 31, 43

Land Army (Britain) 26, 27
League of Nations 50
Leningrad, siege of 20–1

MacArthur, General Douglas 22
Maginot Line 8, 9
Montgomery, General 16, 17

naval combat 14–15, 28
Netherlands 7, 8
New Guinea 30–1
New Zealand 42
North Africa 16–17

Pacific, war in the 14–15, 28–9, 30
Pearl Harbor 14–15
Philippines 22–3
Phoney War 4, 8
Poland 4, 8

Rommel, General Erwin 9, 16
Roosevelt, Franklin 14, 44

Singapore 18–19
Solomon Islands 28
Soviet Union 5, 20–1, 32, 44, 46
Stalin, Joseph 44, 45
submarine warfare 24

United Nations 44, 50, 51
United States 4, 5, 14–15, 22, 24, 28, 30,
    34, 36, 38, 42, 44, 48

women in the war 26–7
World War I 4, 50
World War II
    human and economic costs 4, 20, 40,
        48, 50
    onset of 4
    victory in Europe 5, 46–7

Yalta conference 44–5